JUST TALK THERAPY

SESSIONS WITH YOUNG KIDS (AGES 6-12 YEARS)

HINA BEG

INDIA • SINGAPORE • MALAYSIA

Notion Press

Old No. 38, New No. 6
McNichols Road, Chetpet
Chennai - 600 031

First Published by Notion Press 2019

ISBN 978-1-64678-810-1

I dedicate this book to my ***parents.***

CONTENTS

PREFACE

My Journey

My name is Mrs. Hina Beg. I have been a Counsellor and Psychotherapist since more than a decade. To be more precise, I am a Solution Therapist, which in simple words means that I resolve issues in a short framework of time. Before I share my perspective with you all, I have highlighted some key aspects of my journey below.

My parents are my backbone and they laid the strong foundation that I grew up with. The values and beliefs they instilled within me have made me who I am right now. My two siblings are there to keep a check on me with a smile (the lesser said the better ha! ha! ha!). My husband and my two kids are my strength. I am a happy go lucky person with no grudges in life and feel blessed for everything and to everyone who crossed my path of life.

Since my college days, I found myself with people who shared their life experiences with me. I am a good listener. As a Counsellor, this is the key trait one must possess. I believe in the NOW, the present moment and work with my clients with this belief, to help them bounce back in life resolving the issues that bothered them. I am an empathetic and responsible therapist. My keen interest is in the wellbeing of those who visit me, as *mental health* directly affects one's physical and social wellbeing. As a person, I believe that life is very simple. The demanding timeline we are currently living in is challenging. I hope this attempt to share the views of a therapist will give you a window of hope. In a counselling session only talking is done, situations are analysed and solutions are chalked out to try in the real world. A plethora of options are arranged on a platter by and for the clients so that when any demanding situation comes they know how to get through it. During my journey, I came across individuals who just needed space to share what was on their mind, without being judged. Thus, if one finds themselves stuck in life, where something is bothering them consciously or subconsciously for many days, then one should seek some help. Do not procrastinate the issues until they reach a point where your wellbeing is affected. Your professional and personal life will feel the repercussions if this aspect is left unattended. So be aware and mindful.

This book has many Parts dealing with respective age groups and it will let you peek inside the Session scenario in Counselling. Hence, my journey begins with all my knowledge and wisdom. *Therapeutic Counselling is a temporary phase with a positive outcome.*

ACKNOWLEDGEMENTS

I would like to thank

Ms Hiba Khan my motivator, proof reader and guide

Ms Samawiyah Ulde my proof reader and huge support

Master Faiz Khan who encouraged me and kept a check on my progress

ABOUT THE AUTHOR

Hina Beg is an Entrepreneur and a Psychotherapist. To be precise she is a Solution Therapist, who resolves cases in short span of time. She loves to help people and always strives to assess clients in accordance with professional practice standard and code of ethics. She has experience of Personal (one to one) Counselling and Telephonic Counselling, since more than a decade and has worked with all age groups undergoing various challenges in life. The techniques used by her is as per her clients' needs. Especially when dealing with kids, she is very creative and uses storytelling, drawing, role play etc. She has also conducted interactive workshops on issues like anxiety, anger, bereavement etc. She has good communication skills and connects with her clients with ease. Her aim is to equip the clients with confidence and encourage them to appreciate their true potential.

COUNSELLING IN INDIA

As I snuggle comfortably on my couch with a blank screen glaring in front of me, to pen down my views and experiences as a Therapist, I realize I am blessed to have touched so many lives in such a short time. Sipping my hot coffee, I reflect and encapsulate my thoughts. So here I am!

Counselling in India is very different from what we read in books, mostly having the backdrop or environment which is nothing like the one in India. The intricate beautiful fabric in our society makes counselling an underestimated procedure. There is a taboo to seek out professional help, but what is more noticeable to me, is that everyone already has a counsellor in their family. The setup of a joint family incorporates such counsellors in the form of aunts, uncles or grandparents. Though the concept of joint family has more pros than cons, there is a shift in the society from joint to a nuclear family which is making things go haywire. This inevitable shift is making society amorphous and jittery.

The nagging behaviour of any one relative, the unannounced arrival of someone, the inquisitiveness of elders, the never-ending plans to visit someone or somewhere or get together on every trivial decision or discussion; all these and many more kept the families and society intact. Yes! It did call for a lot of adjustments and caused upheaval but so what!! It also gave amazing memories and experiences filled with laughter and joyful tears. After all, this is what life is all about.

Moving fast forward to this moment, things are different. For me as a Solution Therapist, I find insecurities and too much pressure built into every emotional aspect in society. Survival skills are challenged and thus the healthy mind is always under scrutiny. I have developed my own style, strategies, and adaptation skills when I am addressing my clients. Clients range from kids to adults and so no one technique can be implemented or followed. The diverse background of the clientele allows me to apply a mix and match approach unique to each one. Each client has their own thought process and personality. They are valued for who they are. Having said that, I would now like to draw your attention to what *"Psychotherapy"* actually is.

PSYCHOTHERAPY

Psychotherapy, of course, when Googled will have a hoard of meanings and explanations. But based on my experience, I hold a much more concise view of it. It is the simplest therapy and is commonly known as 'Talk Therapy'. In this the clients are allotted time, usually 50 minutes – 1 hour, where they come and just talk in a safe environment. The sessions are once a week or the frequency is mutually agreed upon depending on the situation. The relationship between the clients and the therapist is of trust and confidentiality. Psychotherapy is a process which if done earnestly helps the clients to bounce back in life in a short span of time. It works best when the clients can do the homework given to them on time. For me, I try to inculcate strength-based counselling and make the process quicker, instilling confidence and adaptability. Once the last session is reached the clients have learned the coping skills and have been made aware of their strengths. To date, ninety-five percent of my cases have been resolved in less than seven sessions. The rest did not continue due to reasons known to them. I respect their decisions and pray for them. As a therapist I maintain my professionalism.

ISSUES PREVALENT IN THE SOCIETY

The society these days is plagued with many mental health issues. I have listed some of them below:

- Depression
- Sadness
- Stress
- Anger Issues
- Suicidal Tendencies
- Marital Disputes
- Sibling Jealousy
- Death Related Worry
- Panic Attacks
- Anxiety
- Focus Related Issues
- Bullying at Schools
- Mobile Addiction
- Loneliness
- Low Self-confidence
- Worthlessness
- Over-Expectations
- Hyperactivity
- Work Management

The list is long and very dynamic. The intensity of each issue may vary, as we are humans. We are complex in our interpretation and understanding. Clients at times have more than two issues that they would like to address.

During Counselling, the first Session is the time when all the concerns and reasons for seeking counselling are discussed. This session takes note of the issues one is facing and trying to manage. Sometimes unresolved issues from the past are the reasons for current discord in one's life. Sometimes a simple thing like *'I cannot say no'* starts bothering a person so much that it weighs on them, leading to stress and health-related issues. Coming to counselling does not mean that one has any mental ailment, it is just a coping platform to unwind and think coherently. It is to discover one's abilities to multitask in their real-life with ease. It is a temporary phase to upgrade oneself personally.

I conduct small workshops on issues like anger, anxiety, expectations, time management, bereavement, etc. These workshops are interactive and result oriented. They are usually held for two days in a row. On the first day after the discussion is over and once the participants reach home; they may have several questions cropping up in their minds. The next day when they attend the workshop, these queries are discussed healthily. The group works on trust and with an agenda to benefit themselves and be beneficial to others in the group too.

I counsel clients through Personal Counselling (one-one) and Telephonic Counselling (only audio medium).

CLIENT WORLD

The clients come from all walks of life and all age groups. The issues as mentioned earlier were, and are to date, very common nationally and globally. I admire each client for their courage to come forward and talk about themselves. It is not an easy task, but once a decision is taken to move forward this is the most rewarding path. Striking a conversation has never been an issue for me. Some clients are scared, broken, scarred, dazed, doubtful, while others may be confused, eager, remote, aggressive, etc. The way they carry themselves varies as per their circumstances. Each reacting as per their situations. *In whatever state they come, they have hope.* They have done the best within their capacity to deal with their issues on their own. Their efforts are always appreciated by me and they are fighters in their own ways. Sitting in front of me is a big thing. Their thoughts are creating riots in their minds and in all this mayhem, to trust someone, is the biggest challenge they undertake. They are given assurance that whatever they share or we discuss is limited to the four walls of the room. No one will ever know about the conversation. This builds the trust part. If kids are accompanied by their guardians or parents, then it is firmly informed that they should not probe the child about anything happening during the sessions. They are told to maintain patience and trust the process. The results will be visible in the child in due course of time. This, I know, is very difficult for them, reasons being obvious—***parents are parents!*** There is this fear in parents which I understand, that what and how much kids will share with me. It is their genuine concern that their children share secrets, including but not limited to the intimate details of each member at home. I, as a therapist, can say with utmost assurance that for me the kid is more important at that point. The details of the family are safe. Every family is doing their best in the ways they know how to. The parent/s are involved in the Counselling process if needed. The idea is to help the child, and we work as a team. Each one has trusted and found their loved ones back and the issues were resolved.

This is a book to share what happens in these counselling sessions. I have divided the book into parts. This is Part 1, a book wherein I have shared the journey of kids (6 years–12 years) attending sessions with me, highlighting my way of therapy and healing of the unconscious mind. The technical unfolding of therapy has been avoided. The purpose is not to teach or to preach- it is just to take you through my experience as a Counsellor and Psychotherapist. My views on many cases can be construed as subjective ones, for the simple fact that most things usually are, and that in the world of psychology there is a high level of flexibility. Here, I do not refer to any specific case, but a compilation of the process that worked for me while dealing with kids. Go ahead and read.

KIDS THERAPY: AGES 6–12 YEARS

When kids suddenly become quiet, hyperactive, aggressive, angry, sad, etc. their daily routine gets hampered. Initially, it is ignored and not noticeable, neither at home nor in school. The change is gradual and it starts affecting the kids' behaviour slowly. As this is left unattended, in due course of time the kids' academics and social interaction start to decline. The parents now start to get worried as they are unable to handle the change. The parents are stressed out as the kids are not reachable. The kids refuse to share or talk about what is going on in their minds. At this point, when the parents have done their best they consider taking some professional help. They contact me to make an appointment and come to the clinic at the given day and time.

Before Counselling with the kid begins, I have a brief conversation with the parents and the kid together, after which I advise the parents to wait outside or come and fetch their kid after an hour since the session lasts for about an hour. The kids, once alone, are very conscious and alert. To make them comfortable I always have some blank pages and colours for them to scribble and draw. This helps the kids ease down and the process of Counselling starts. Drawing is a non-invasive and non-verbal tool that calms the mind. Gradually the kids start to unwind and the body posture relaxes. Usually, with kids my approach is using techniques like drawing, storytelling, talking about comic characters, games, sports, riddles, role play, etc. I keep myself updated on these topics. Through different tools, it is usually easy for the kids to talk about issues they are dealing with. Though not in specific words, but it is enough for me to identify and give a direction to counselling. Each and every query they ask during their session is addressed. They start sharing their thoughts and the process cruises through with my guidance, along with appropriate words or desired discussions. This helps in rapport building and trust is built in the process. When the session is about to end we start closing on a positive note, recapping on certain points and few tips are reiterated- which they may use throughout the week if the need arises. Homework (colouring/drawing one page every day until the next session) is discussed with the kid. I tell them that the homework could be done before sleeping or when they are anxious, angry, upset, sad etc. The kid is enthusiastic to do the homework and promises the same, blurting out a *'done, ma'am!'* instantly.

Parents are called in. They wait outside eagerly to know if all went well. Signalling reassurance to calm the concerned parents, the session comes to an end. I discuss with the parent/s about their kid's diet and meal timing. At this point, the kid at times interrupts our conversation, sharing that *'mom always says no to junk food'*. Then the explanations from the mom follow, and to diffuse such situations we talk about food likings and preferences. Some changes in the diet are made. After mutual agreement with the kid, the menu is decided. The consensus is reached and both, the mom and the kid, are satisfied. I even ask the parent to get Vitamin D and Vitamin B12 tested in their next routine medical check-up. If the kid is in an extremely gloomy mood, sad or very low in energy then the tests are advised to be done on a priority basis. Games and family time are also given as homework to the parents. And...at that point one can see the kid's eyes gleaming with joy and their face lit up.

The sessions are scheduled once a week, preferably on the same day and time. The kids come with their drawings, some are very particular while some casual about it. Homework given to the parents is also sometimes done and sometimes not. That is okay with me, awareness and acceptance leading to action is a gradual process. Kids wait outside as sometimes parents want to share their experience throughout the week. Once done quickly, the parents are once again advised either to pick them up after an hour or wait outside. The kid enters the room when the parents leave the room. They are eager to share their drawings and before even asking I am staring at the pages with colours. I go through their drawings- page-wise, taking time to see their efforts. The kid asks softly '*do you like it?*' my eyes sparkle and they smile back. When I praise their drawing, and usually their quick response is, '*Oh! This I drew when I was tired and it is not so good*'. I just listen and encourage them to speak about it. They are surprised to know how their scribbling is so awesome. Once all drawings are scanned, either I ask them to tell a story on any one of their drawings, or I initiate a story choosing any one of their drawings and they follow. Their views are very interesting- sometimes I oppose them and give my magical angle to it. The kids defend their ideas or accept my ideas in the ongoing story. The room is charged and they are all in an active mode. The thinking is fast and the speed of conversation escalates. I am observant of the small changes in their body language, eye movement, tone, choice of words, accent, etc. All this happens rapidly and simultaneously. Giving them space and appreciating everything they share is very important throughout the session. Sometimes, while narrating the story, they end up calling themselves stupid. I smile, react with my facial expressions which the kids are quick to pick. By now they know that everything is possible in the stories we share in this room. There are no boundaries and the kid is permitted to speak out freely. When they falter and go against the ideal set notion they need validation. They glance at me, especially when they introduce a new concept in their drawing. They have my approval and so they confidently continue talking. Each drawing is discussed in detail. If I notice any movement in them, I take the process forward and drift their attention to their real-life scenario. Home, play area, school, garden, market, relatives, friends are some of the areas they want to talk about. Especially friends. We briefly talk about their interest and make a deal to discuss about it in the next session. We also keep a nickname for this deal and it is a secret. The session ends on a note of positivity and again the same drawing homework is given. When the parents come in to fetch the kid, the nickname is mentioned by us with a wink, high five or a thumbs-up gesture. The parents are clueless and surprised. The kid, with an ear to ear smile, says, *'nothing mom, it's our secret'*, and they leave.

During the third session, the kid is in a better state. The shift usually happens. The drawings are scanned and discussed if needed. This session is our secret session. The kid is enthusiastic and reminds me of- *'ma'am, remember'*. My big nod encourages them, and they start talking about the areas that are confusing or upsetting them. The areas could be their friends, family, teachers, building friends, etc. We spend time talking about it in detail and I share a few tricks with them which they may adopt and try. The tricks are suggested keeping in mind the kid's coping skills, strengths, likings and enthusiasm. If I observe that the situation is the same or if the kid is silent, we slow down and revisit the last story mentioned in the previous session. If the kid has progressed forward, we move ahead and usually by this session the kid bounces back. The situations in their life that are related to them are talked about in detail. The kid is inquisitive and has queries about many topics, jumping from one to the other in a *zigzag* manner. They find answers and eventually can join the dots which are laid in front of them. Everything is synchronized in some structural way. Homework is given once more. Storytelling is always a part of the session.

The next session is a testing one. Usually, it is seen that the kids have done one or two drawings, and at times these drawings are done just before coming for the session or the night before. The drawings are scanned casually and storytelling is done. The kids are full of energy while sharing their likes from sports to cartoon characters- the rapport building is now very fast. The topics are no longer disconnected- they are just shared with great speed. The thoughts are more coherent. The kid shares how he/ she tried to implement the tips during the week. They share their experience with honesty- even if they tried a particular tip but it did not give the desired result. We work on that, coming up with more options, sometimes with crazy solutions that revive the kid's spirit. There are times when they don't believe in themselves or the solution, but I tell them to give it a shot nonetheless. Usually, they accept it with conviction. Time flies and the session ends with a note that the next session is the last one. The kid usually does not react to this, but when they are told that the drawing homework is optional this time they are happy.

The closure session is important. It is during this session that we go through the disturbing or upsetting issues that they came with. Together we scan the journey. I observe the facial expressions, non-verbal movements and the pace of the conversation. At any point in time, if I feel that something is amiss, we spend time on it, referring to previous drawings, connecting them with the current discussion. The kids share their experience of the previous week with the new tip they had applied. It worked for them and they even invented new tips while dealing with their situation! This is always praised and I always congratulate them for such an achievement. The session ends with a big smile. The kids are happy and full of life. The parents are happy too.

Parents play a major role in child therapy. Probing is not allowed- to which they agree. After two sessions, the parents start participating and do their bit. They are advised that certain words or statements are to be avoided when interacting with their kids. Diet is again emphasized. *I strongly recommend a whiteboard with coloured markers to all the parents.* This is an important medium to communicate, motivate and have a fun time with their kid. Parents are informed of things they may try with their routine, to bond with their kids.

Usually, in this busy life, parents are trying to earn and make both ends meet. The time to have a chat with their kids is missing. The kids end up only receiving orders and pushed from one class to the other. It is like a checklist of some manual which comes with a product. This list is a bit thawed during the sessions. Despite having hectic schedules, the commands are converted to conversations. Ways are made possible to connect with these beautiful young minds. ***Kids are our future generation. One should strive to give them memories and not data.*** The moments are to be filled with laughter, appreciation, smiles, surprises and understanding. These moments form the kids' memories.

Trust your kids and be a good role model- is the ultimate tip for parents.

MY ANALYSIS AND CONCLUSION

Kids, as I have mentioned previously, come to Counselling once the parents or guardians notice some behavioural changes in them. When they are sitting in front of me for the first session, they are clueless. Some are just accompanying their parents, unaware that they are coming to a therapist (At times the kids don't know what a *Therapist* or *Counsellor* means). That is okay, as when the appointment is taken how to bring the kid for counselling this is addressed. The parents don't know how to tell their kids. So I suggest what can be done, taking into account the case and the child's nature.

Once in the room, I first speak to the child. I explain to him/her why he/she is here and what will happen in the sessions. I let them know that it is only talk therapy and the parents are sitting just outside. They are usually okay with the arrangement and at times some even want to make sure the door is closed properly. Some scan the room to make themselves aware of their surroundings. Some sit quietly in a pensive mood. Sometimes they are even angry, as the time they are spending with me is usually their playtime. They do share that all the kids must be enjoying elsewhere while they are sitting in this room. This is a very important point. This is the first thing we talk about. Thus the session begins.

Kids usually are not aware of the issues which hamper their happiness or their current behavioural changes. It is very difficult for them to know the real reasons leading to their sadness, anger, aggression, etc. Through Counselling Sessions and their homework which is done regularly, this process is addressed. During the session there is no labelling, no judgment passed or any concept of wrong or right raised. They are young kids; space is given to them so that they can talk freely without any inhibitions. They are allowed to say or express their emotions, which are monitored by me. Channelling their energy on options that best suit their circumstances is done throughout the sessions. Kids feel their value, start appreciating views of others and look forward to implementing discussed ideas in their real life.

Although I am not a trained art therapist, I can say that I do fair justice to art as a form of expression. The kids are asked to colour or draw directly using crayons (oil pastels). Each drawing is given some time of speculation. The kids are told to randomly select any drawing (or I choose one of their drawings) and then I ask them to narrate a story around it. Drawing helps the kids to ease down. It brings peace and calms the agitated mind. It is a form where we explore the turmoil the kids go through. It is the safest mode to connect the conscious and subconscious mind. The kids feel in control- that they are the master of their own lives- and use any colour or shape to express themselves at that given point. It gives them personal independence. The stories knitted around the drawings help give a voice to what they intend to share. This is a careful process. The rhythm has to be maintained as we know that kids are very expressive when it comes to *their* storytelling. At times I notice certain areas that need more attention. The twists in stories and games help address those areas. Sometimes I challenge them in their own stories, keeping in mind the details about them, I counter play what I feel. This at times brings out another side of them which is very innovative and creative.

Kids love to talk about the topics which interest them. This is natural and holds valid for all age groups. The only difference with kids is that they share without any restrictions. I participate with equal enthusiasm and interest. Conscious efforts are made to visit the issues pertaining to therapy and checking their coping skills. The kids are shocked and delighted when they find out that I play games and have knowledge about the characters they are referring to. I keep myself updated and love to know their world so it is very crucial for me to be aware of the world of sports, games, video games, cartoon characters, stories, riddles, etc. that the kids of this group indulge in.

When dealing with this age group special care is taken. Any informed suggestion, if given, is tapered down to their age. As the session progresses, the kids blurt out many options that could be suited to tackle different situations. Together we role model certain situations to see if the kid can select the right one. This inculcates confidence in kids. The inquisitiveness in kids leads them to ask many questions. We have a quick rapport-building up. Each session helps resolve the very purpose of why they are here. They have mixed feelings when it is time for them to leave. It is okay to some, while for some it matters a lot. They are given assurance that they may come to meet me whenever they feel like. I am always there, they may send me their drawings and I will reply; with this, they are quick to shift their mood back to being chirpy.

I hope this book sheds some light on what the procedure is like. It is safe, beneficial, and trustworthy and helps the child cross the unknown hurdle in life with ease. This is solely the way I work. I avoid using technical terms as the result is simple. Each therapist has their own style and way of approaching the sessions they undertake. I focus on using different techniques as per the client. The idea is to instil problem-solving skills and enable the kids to hold a positive attitude in life. Once the sessions are complete the kid learns how to express and communicate emotions in healthy ways. It is okay to revisit after a year for a session or two. This is fine, as at times with growing pressure and too much work, parents may have that concern that their child might slip into their previous state. So, just like any annual health check-up, a visit to the therapist is not a bad idea. The crux is that the child should be happy and able to manage their situations with ease. The feedback I had from parents always brings a smile and a silent pray for these sweet souls. I hope to make a difference in this demanding society in my own little creative ways.

JOURNEY WITH THE CLIENT

Here, I have tried to share with my readers the journey with a client named Hero. I have tried to give a realistic picture of the sessions with the boy. The approach I adopt depends on the client. It is casual, observant, simple and often good-humoured. The idea is to be with the client and cruise him to bounce back in life. His verbal and non-verbal form of communication is observed and the sessions progress accordingly. I have also shared with you the contribution of a good diet to young minds, and what one may include as a part of each meal. One may be more creative and add whatever they prefer. The idea is to give a balanced and appealing diet.

The kids and parents work together as a team to gift peace and happiness to their kids. The therapy actually happens between sessions, that is why it is scheduled on the same day and time, and it is an ongoing process. Thus, ***"Talk Therapy"*** is a therapy that is dynamic, full of positivity and is constructive.

SESSIONS WITH A BOY

Appointment time – 5:00 pm

Name of the boy – Hero

Age – 8 years

SESSION 1

The bell rings; the receptionist informs me that clients have come. I ask her to send them in. There is a hesitant knock at the door.

"Come in!"

They entered and the boy was accompanied by both his parents. While they made themselves comfortable, I noticed that the boy was upset about something. He was very stiff and just sat there with a grim look. In the meantime, the parents greeted and an exchange of names took place.

"He is not studying these days", blurted the mother.

"Not listening to me and doing his work", added the dad.

The boy kept still, staring the floor.

The desperation to just see their kids obeying their commands was too apparent. The glances they gave to the kid were rapid- as if to check his response.

"Ok, so is this what you want from your kid? To study and to listen to you" I enquired gently.

Their instant joint reply was "yes". Before I could speak any further, they started speaking, overlapping each other's statements, sharing how their son was a good student and had suddenly lost interest in studies. The boy stole glances at his parents with quick blank looks. He was surely searching for something but did not say anything. I noticed him as I spoke with his parents. After they were done with their bit, I asked the child if he was aware of what Counselling was all about.

He just gazed at me silently.

"Hero, do you know what Counselling is all about?" I asked softly.

He suddenly said, "No, and I only came because my parents asked me to."

"Okay, and why do you think your parents asked you to come here?"

"Only they know; they never told me," he was quick to add.

"You don't listen to us, Hero, so we had to come here," snapped the dad. At this point, I calmly explained what counselling was all about, to Hero and his parents.

"It is a Talk Therapy, where you will be coming to see me once a week and each session will last for about an hour. Hero, we will have some fun talk about games and your mom and dad will not be a part of it." This did catch his attention as he looked at me to know more. I just nodded and addressed his parents- "Kindly do not ask your son about what happens in the sessions as it will be our talk. I will appreciate the patience you both will show and your trust in your son."

I had already briefed them about the procedure over a phone call, but made sure I said it once again in front of the child. It was important. Although they looked doubtful, they agreed. I told them to relax and not to worry- “We all will work together as a team.” The boy did smile as I uttered the word ‘team’, and it was easy to see why. His parents in a game. Ah! Very difficult to play on then. Leaving him with his thoughts I advised the parents to either sit outside and wait, or they could come after an hour to fetch him. They left, giving some quick tips to their child to be good.

“Please close the door, Hero”

He silently got up and closed the door and sat down. He examined his surroundings as if to check if all was in place. I slipped a blank page towards him and kept some colours alongside.

“Do you know how to draw a mountain?” I asked.

“Yeah, that’s easy, but I don’t like to sketch,” he answered.

“Sketch? Yeah, that’s very time consuming- some people are very good at it- I agree with you- even I am not fond of sketching”, I said softly.

“Really? There... the mountains are here what else...”

As he was absorbed in drawing and colouring the mountains I asked him to add a hut, trees and anything he likes to draw and told him that there are no colour restrictions. He was quick to try different colours. Once he was done with his colouring he looked at me and said, “You know, I am very angry,” before I could react, he continued. “This is my playing time. My mom and dad just ordered me to come here. I hate them. All my friends must be playing and we had a match today”.

It is natural for anyone to be upset when their free time is compromised. Hero had a match, and to not be there was actually worth his anger. He had no choice but to listen to his parents. If we ponder on this, it was his responsibility to be a part of the team and execute his role in the game. When kids play, we take it as just a time pass which makes us behave in the way we do. Calling them in the middle of the game, giving them warnings that if a particular task is not done then they will not be going to play or even allowing them to play beyond the allotted time, just because they (parents) had friends coming over or they (parents) had to go somewhere. Whatever the case, there are reasons why I maintain that game time is important.

Let us evaluate the impact of each scenario.

Situation 1: Calling them in the middle of the game

If this happens once in a while then it is okay. But if it is more than that then it needs some attention. My focus is on the kid. Let's say the game is football, which is a team game. The kids work really hard to be in the team which may even have kids who are older to him and they may be bossy. So to be with them and deal with the situation is not easy. Yet, for kids, being a part of the team is the only thing that's on their mind. They will do anything to be there and they succeed. So, while games seem like a simple matter to us, they are not easy actually. It is a learning process. After they work so hard and eventually get a chance to play, to leave the game is very difficult and upsetting. It leads to anger and aggression. Other aspects of their life, including studies, will face its repercussions.

Situation 2: Giving them warnings

When parents use game time as bait or a warning tool so that the kids finish their work or listen to them then it again needs some introspection. Once in a while is fine, but if it is repetitive then one has to be careful with it. The kids have school, tuition, rest and play as major chunks of a day. The playtime is gradually shrinking due to social pressure. *Your kid has not joined karate, dance class, drawing, music...?* Is it needed? Just because the kid happened to mention that he/she likes to dance, lo and behold! It is held so closely by the parents that they will start inquiring about it. They make sure that the kid joins the best; drop and pick up is arranged; the kid is now in a time-bound and space-bound class. Kids usually like the classes initially, some are keen about it- but not all. Slowly the enthusiasm fades. Parents are now more insistent; they have invested themselves emotionally in these classes. So they start giving warning to the kids- they will not go to a birthday party if they miss these specific classes or the time with society kids will be denied. *Do you see what is happening now?* The kids start disliking a rigid structure. This slowly creeps into the educational setup too, and the focus towards studying declines, as this same warning is used for studies and completing homework.

Situation 3: More time given because parents are busy

When parents are busy, have their friends coming over or they have to go somewhere, then they do try to shower extra love and concern on their kids. They give them extra time to go and play or spend time with their friends. This may seem harmless but the catch is the next day- when the kids are reminded of these so-called favours that were bestowed upon them by their parents. So now they have to listen to them and pay a price. Obviously, this is not the right thing to do since this extra time was probably not even asked for by the kids! They are quick to learn how to manipulate their needs and make use of these moments to their benefit. The next time this ordeal will disturb them for sure, but slowly they will get used to the routine and the scolding will not matter to them so much.

There are many such situations that families go through. This is just the tip of the iceberg. In all of the above situations, the kids will not be able to rationalize what is expected of them- it will only resonate with them as orders. The kids simply need free time without any strings attached. It is the time where they learn to be responsible and make their own decisions. Parents should appreciate their kids' needs and be involved in what they tell; listen to each detail they share even if it is as trivial as the kid saying that today he went to fetch the ball.

Hero cleared his throat and took permission to drink water. He carried a water bottle with him.

"A match! Which sport? That sounds interesting," I said

"Yes, but now I will miss it," he said softly.

"I am so sorry you had to miss it, Hero. Next time we will plan your session time according to *your* schedule."

"Really? Its football, and you know- I am a very good goalkeeper!" he said in excitement.

"Oh, that's awesome! That's such an important position in a team. You are strong and what is the name of your team... By the way, how will your team manage today? Do you want to go now?" I asked him.

He checked his watch quickly and said, "Not possible, now it is too late. They will manage as one of my Block D friends also plays as a goalkeeper, he will get a chance today," he sighed heavily. The sacrifice was big for his age. I asked his schedule for the week and the day he was free so that we could plan accordingly. I was not surprised to hear that it was a very tight schedule- back to back classes- and only this short window of playing with friends in between, which was obviously important to him. The importance of it is so obvious when you listen to the kids and how passionate they are about their friends and the time they spend with them. They fight, unite and enjoy each moment without any expectations. Time flies and they end up saying *'abhi to aaya tha'*.

"So you like football and-" he quickly completed the sentence, "- sleeping, but I don't get enough time to sleep as every day I have to go to school." "Wow, every day! That's amazing."

He was surprised and started to relax in his chair. This seems to be of some interest to him. I asked him to imagine what it would be like if he had to skip school for an entire week. He was instantly very happy with that thought. I observed the shift in his body posture. He now folded his legs and sat on the chair, ready to roll out his plans. The voice gained a pitch but in no time he fell quiet. Silence in the room; I waited patiently. After some time, he asked me, "Is it actually possible? I can miss school... and maybe that boring drawing class too?" I nodded and asked him to imagine, at least. We started the day one- with lots of sleep and eating, and he said he will chill in front of the TV. The second day was also similar- he will go down to play and once home will chill and eat. The third-day plan was about to start when he said he does not want to miss so many days. He loves to meet his school friends and would not like to miss his sports period as they were having some inter-house competition coming up. I said okay, and asked him to revisit his first two days of not going to school. We started all over again, slowly monitoring the timeline versus his activity. I even asked him about the timetable of that particular day. We discussed study subjects and his look changed. He was serious and tried to control his emotions as he spoke about his subjects. I drew his attention to his drawing, asking him to narrate a story around it. I initiated the first line in the usual way. *'Once upon a time'*. He followed and started his story, "Once upon a time there were mountains and the sun was about to set. In this red hut lived an old man with his grandson." At this point, I interjected and asked softly- What is the name of the grandson? He had no answer as this was a story, he said. I encouraged him to give the boy some name, something special. I gave him a few random names- How about football? Gems? Rocket? Net? - and each time he would just shake his head and laugh.

Finally, he said, "Okay, the boy's name is Dumbo and grandfather's name is Rambo."

"Interesting, so the boy loves the elephant with those huge ears?" I asked softly.

He looked with eyes wide open as indeed- he loved Dumbo. Hero loved the book, the Disney classic, 'Dumbo'.

We both struck a chord and he kept on talking about the boy, Dumbo, in his drawing. Time was ticking fast. We only spoke about the drawing and made a story on it. Hero explained how Dumbo had to go to school early morning, though he was lazy at times, but the thought of meeting and talking to his friends charged him. Slowly, the shift was made in monosyllables from the story to real life. The importance of school, friends, studies, rest, society friends, food, among other things, is just scraped through. I did not delve too much into details as I could see that Hero was not comfortable with a particular topic whenever school was referred. I kept it to myself at this point. Hero also said that Dumbo was sad at times and sat under the tree with his books. I gave a magic twist to the story and soon the grass turned into jelly, the tree could talk, the flowers grew huge and the hut was glowing. Hero's eyes twinkled with excitement. I took a U-turn and talked about the inter-house event that was going to take place in his school.

He said, "Football, and I am the goalkeeper in my house team also."

"What will happen if you miss your school? Do you have an equally good goalie in your house?" I enquired.

His silence answered my query. I continued and drew his attention to how talented he was. He was good at his studies, sports and the teachers really trusted him. His house needs him to be in school every day and be fit. I drifted the topic from classroom to football. He loved Ronaldo, so I shared some facts about him. How discipline he is and to play like him one needs to work regularly, and of course one cannot talk about Ronaldo without mentioning his famous kicks. At this point, attention was drawn to the drawing again. It was dark by now and it was sleep time; both Rambo and Dumbo were asleep. With this, the story ended for the day and Hero again took permission to drink water, after which we recapped the main jumping points of the session. The phone bell rang, breaking the harmony of the room. I was informed that the parents were waiting outside.

I asked Hero when he would be able to visit in the coming week. He thought for some time and juggled his schedule with deftness. Wednesday, came the answer. I agreed and called his parents inside. Hero was happy to see them.

I asked the parent to be seated (The drawing is removed and kept safely in my drawer).

They looked calmer by now. I emphasized that they should not enquire about what happened in the session. They just needed to trust the process. I shared with them that Hero may need only four to five sessions; he is a smart kid and they are lucky to have him as their son.

I asked them about their meal timings and what they generally had for breakfast. The breakfast was the toughest task, the dinner was late and lunchtime was very casual.

Hero quickly said, "My mom always gives me the same food every day and my dad has BP, so no junk for me too."

"Did we not take you out on Sunday?" the dad replied (today was Thursday) as if his son mentioning it to me made it seem like they are stringent and don't take his son out for meals.

I gave a nod to Hero; he was quick to understand. I asked them to make a deal with each other. This was the homework for the parents. It was a team task. Everyone had to give their food options, Hero would make a list and then after everyone's approval a menu timetable would be made for breakfast, lunch and dinner for the entire week, at least until the next session. It was easy and they all agreed. The boy had all his choices spilling out of his mouth and I smiled. The guidelines were that the menu had to be colourful, healthy, and interesting- a bit of junk food was allowed.

The homework for Hero was that he had to colour one page every day using oil pastel crayons. No pencil, ruler, or pen was allowed. Only freehand drawing and colouring. In his next session, he will come with his drawing book. I asked the parents to come for the next session on Wednesday. Hero smiled and in the meantime, his mom said she will check his son's schedule and confirm. I agreed, but before anything further could be said, Hero said softly, "Mom, on Wednesday I have no classes." In no time the next session was confirmed. To see their son smiling and confirming another session did surprise them. They did not say anything, the exchange of look between the mother and father was enough to suggest the same.

With this, the session ended. The parents left with their son. Hero waved goodbye and closed the door behind him.

I sat there for some time. It is always nice to hear stories and ideas from these amazing kids, full of enthusiasm and passion. I could feel the energy around me even after he had left.

The Meal Plan

"Eat Breakfast Like a King, Lunch Like a Prince, and Dinner Like a Pauper"

The famous saying still holds good. During breakfast, the body is ready to absorb nutrients effectively. Eating breakfast rich in protein and fibre is best advised. A quick snack at recess time, replenishes the energy needed by the body which lasts until lunchtime.

I prefer quick, easy and less cooking time-consuming food. So, below is what comes to my mind right away. Mix and match, innovate, add, delete and be flexible. The crux is to give a *balanced diet* and the meal in an appealing way *with a smile.* Kids' likes and dislikes should be borne in mind and tackled accordingly.

A quick look at what a balanced diet means: '*A balanced diet is a diet which includes different types of food that provide adequate amount of nutrients to maintain good health*'

The Food Groups and Nutrient Groups are nothing but grouping the foods which provide similar nutrients and cater to specific needs of our body. The idea is to consume food from each group according to our age and our body requirement.

The groups which we all are aware of are:

1. Carbohydrates- this provides us with energy. It gives the kids the boost they need to perform activities throughout the day. The high metabolism

has to be taken care of. The energy from sweet products needs to be monitored.

Food rich in carbohydrates- Bread, Pasta, Cereals, Rice, Potatoes, Noodles, etc.

2. Protein- this helps in the building and repairing of tissues in our body, for example, our muscles, hair, bone, and skin are all dependent on protein. Protein also assists in various reactions in our body. It takes care of our growth and this is especially important at a young age. Thus foods rich in protein should be included in the diet daily.

   Food rich in Protein- Eggs, Meat, Poultry, Fish, Beans, Peas, Soybean, Dal (lentils), Dairy products, cheese, etc.

3. Fats- this is a backup reserve of energy for our body in case carbohydrates are absent. It helps certain vitamins to be absorbed by the body and acts as an insulation to our body. Kids need to intake a required amount of fats as they are very active and need twice the amount of energy as compared to adults.

   Food rich in Fats- Whole Milk dairy products, cooking Oil, Meat, Fish, Nuts, Ghee, Vanaspati, Butter, etc.

4. Vitamins and Minerals- these are essential and may not be needed in a macro amount. Small amounts of Vitamins are needed by our body to function properly. They cannot be synthesised by our body and hence it is imperative to consume them through a variety of food throughout the day. On the other hand, Minerals are present in our tissues

and body fluids. Both Vitamins and Minerals are a must for good growth and a healthy body.

Food rich in Vitamins and Minerals- Fruits, Dates, Vegetables, Meat, Eggs, Fortified food available in the market etc.

Why Do I Emphasise on Vitamin D and Vitamin B12?

Some vitamins are very important and are not available through vegetables, thus extra care is taken while planning a menu for kids. Though deficiency is usually observed in adults and happens slowly, in my view these vitamins should not be neglected. Nowadays its deficiency or low counts of these Vitamins is becoming common in younger kids too, as they are now spending more time in sedentary play and inside the house.

Vitamin B12 helps keep the body's nerve and blood cells healthy and helps in the production of DNA in our body. It is found in animal-sourced food like meat, fish, egg and dairy products. Fortified cereals or fortified food products available in the market may contribute to the availability of this vitamin for those who are vegetarians or have low Vitamin B12. Almost all *multivitamins* have Vitamin B12 which may be given as a supplement for a brief period.

The decrease count of Vitamin B12 may lead to lethargy, fatigue, tingling, muscle weakness, numbness, loss of appetite, neurological disorders, constipation, soreness of mouth and tongue, poor memory etc.

Likewise, Vitamin D which is usually a sunshine blessing and is also found in- egg yolk, cod liver oil, and fatty fish. Some food products are fortified with Vitamin

D and may be consumed to meet the nutrient requirement. This Vitamin is also very important as its decrease count may reflect in our body via body aches, cramps, depression, low feeling, dental deformities, etc. It may cause kids to become introverted or aggressive and anxious.

The study on each food component is exhaustive and elaborate. The main thing we need to keep in mind is to give our kids a balanced diet- which is not difficult. I merely wished to share my experience when it comes to Vitamin D and B12, and I have found that most of the time it is just that these Vitamins are below normal counts which hampers the kids' stamina and behaviour. The kids become moody, lethargic, lose interest in the activities they used to love and in general they become grumpy. If a child (or any individual) eats a variety of available foods from each food group mentioned above, in an adequate amount, their body will receive all the nutrients and vitamins required for it to function properly. So, make your diet colourful, interesting and healthy.

Benefits and Options of Food

A) Benefits of eating a healthy breakfast:

- It will boost the kids' attention span, concentration, and memory
- It will enable them to be active listeners in school. The concepts taught in school will be understood well and kids will start enjoying their school
- The kids will be able to manage tasks given to them, their school level skills will be developed better and they will start feeling confident

- It will help the kids to handle pressure and have lower levels of perceived stress.
- The kids will also experience less emotional distress
- Physically, the kids will have good stamina and will be active
- They will have fewer chances of becoming obese

Food that could be given for breakfast to our smart kids:

- Paratha which should be thin rolled up and given with little ketchup, or with a dash of butter
- Pancake with a layer of Nutella and one scoop ice cream
- Potato vegetable and puri
- Plain fresh roti with any vegetable or non-veg gravy
- Cornflakes, milk, and fruit
- Any milkshake, like banana, apple, chocolate, etc. with honey
- Pasta with vegetables and cheese
- Sandwiches
- Bun with butter and boiled egg

B) Benefits of eating Lunch:

- It replenishes the energy needed by the kid and they feel refreshed to take on the few hours ahead of them before the next meal
- The kids' metabolism is active and the kid will feel less lethargic
- The food helps to give the kids' necessary vitamins for the day

- The calories from lunch will enable the kids to reach their growth parameters concerning their age

Food that could be given for lunch to our smart kids:

- Dal (lentils), rice, vegetables/chicken gravy, roti and rice
- Vegetable soup and khichdi (lentil + rice)
- Vegetable pulao
- Pasta with vegetables
- Maggi with vegetables
- Lassi, fresh juice or buttermilk along with their meal
- Homemade pizza or burger

C) Benefits of snacks at tea or snack time / Dunch:

- It provides the kids with energy for the classes they are about to attend
- For those kids who eat less quantity, snack time is a way to ensure that the kids are getting adequate nutrients
- It provides the energy supplement needed so that the kids do not get cranky
- It is also a time to bond with the kids

Food that could be given as snacks to our smart kids:

- Any seasonal fruit
- A cup of milk with few biscuits
- Nuts
- Sandwiches
- Slightly fried and salted makhana (foxnut)
- Any pakora (paneer/potato/onion/mixed vegetable) with a milkshake
- Fresh fruit juice

D) Benefits of Dinner:

- This being the last meal of the day is very important
- It allows the family members to spend quality time together
- The nutrients can be balanced during this mealtime
- It inculcates good value time, eating habits and kids learn from their elders the small etiquettes one should have while being seated in a group

Food that could be given for dinner to our smart kids:

- Depends on the family!

SESSION 2

The Appointment for the second session was decided for Wednesday.

"May I come in, Ma'am?" a familiar voice broke the silence.

"Come in."

As the boy entered holding his drawing book close to his chest, his parents peeped in and said that they would come to fetch him and left closing the door silently.

"Aunty... no, no... miss... I mean, ma'am... see, I have done this yesterday," he fumbled to address me as he was excited to show what he had coloured. He quickly turned the pages and talked at the same time, explaining one drawing and then another. It was hopscotch and there was too much energy in the room. I was quiet with quick fillers so I could match his speed, listening carefully to everything he said. The tone, words, pauses, facial expressions, body language- everything being absorbed by me simultaneously. After some time, he paused for a few minutes.

"Hmm, Hero you have done a great job. Now this drawing- I gestured to the one which was open in front of us and he just stared- is very interesting. Do you think this is a dream of Dumbo?" I spoke softly, placing his last drawing slowly near the drawing book. He glanced at it and back to the page. He stood up for a split moment and then sat back on the chair; took permission to drink water; while sipping water he just looked up. It was as though he trusted me enough to understand what was going through his mind. I truly respect that look.

"You miss him?" I added very softly. He immediately looked at me with stillness. He froze for a moment.

"He loved you a lot. You are lucky," I said.

"Lucky?" he asked in a mixed tone, sipping his water. I just nodded.

"He left me alone so I am not lucky. I miss him." He said it very softly. Tears trickled down his pale cheeks and he just fidgeted with his water bottle. The room was filled with painful silence. I offered him a tissue paper and then picked up a crayon and rolled it towards him, slowly. He traced my movement and said nothing.

"So this is him, right?" He nodded. "Well, let us make this space very, very special." I gradually encouraged him. He kept his water bottle slowly and came forward, thinking in a pensive mood. Picking up the crayon he drew stars around that area; I gave him a few other colours to choose from. He chose blue and started colouring further. "Blue was his favourite colour," he finally said while colouring the page frantically. The rapid movements, expressions, and how his body reacted, all were very important. This happens so quickly that expressing in words does not do justice to what the kid goes through. Once he finished colouring, he looked calmer.

“So many stars! Wow! This is beautiful, it is looking so magical,” I said.

“You know, he used to tell me stories at night and we used to have a great time. Whenever I wanted anything, my dad said no! And he used to give it to me quietly,” he said and looked at me.

“Stories at night, you mean bedtime stories?” He nodded. “So you were lucky...every day a new story. Will you share with me one of your stories? I will feel as if he is here and I also miss my grandparent.” I said. He quickly glanced at me listening intently as I continued “I miss them too. So, Hero, together we will remember them now, okay?” he managed to smile. He asked me if my granddad told me stories. He wanted to know if I was lucky too. I shared with him: “No, not every day. We had a big family and he was busy.” He suddenly told me not to worry- even I was lucky. We both smiled and he shared everything that came to his mind. How he used to disturb him and yet his granddad never complained; the evening strolls with him; the dessert time; and shared many small incidents which he could recall at that point of time. I added mine in between and we laughed at some as we saw the similarity in our pranks. He was much more talkative now. We finally moved from that page to the first one. It had caught my attention since the moment I had seen it. I asked him when he had drawn that- It was after he came from his boring class (remember!). I praised the chaos on the page and asked him to talk about it more. He said that he had been very angry at that time and as I had suggested in the last session, he could draw when he was upset or angry, and so he had done that. Pointing to the page he said after *this* he was not so angry, he took a bath and finished his homework. We spent some time on this anger page and gradually moved on to the next one. Suddenly, he pleaded.

"Please tell my mom and dad, I don't want to go for these classes."

I assured him that I would convey this to them; he need not worry about it.

"Thanks and you know this is Dumbo with his new shoes," he showed me another drawing giving the character a name and we slowly drifted into Hero's world of action, drama, suspense, and I kept on adding twists to it. He sometimes fought, challenged or argued with what I said. I patiently listened to his side and we both mutually agreed at some point. I randomly mentioned his granddad and he included him in the story without any pause.

Today's session was all about dealing with the loss of loved ones. It is not easy for the kids to accept *the loss* by just saying, that it is okay. Many unanswered questions stay with the kids. We discussed it in detail with reasoning, humour, and drawings. Many more thoughts and questions would come to Hero's mind once he reaches home. I will address them in the remaining sessions. Fifteen minutes were left for the session to get over. Just then Hero said that he had gone to school every day, and we both clapped without any sound. He laughed at this new way of clapping, and also told me that they have a new teacher. I could see that he was very happy with this change.

"So your math teacher left?" I asked. He looked surprised but was in too much of a hurry to share the new development and so he skipped my mentioning the subject name.

"Yesss! (With a victory fist) She left and the new teacher is very sweet. She talks so nicely to us and explains everything on the board," he said in one breath and clapped silently. I smiled at him and we spoke about the subject. Just then the telephone bell rang- the receptionist informed me that Hero's parents were waiting outside. They knocked on the door and I asked Hero to sit outside and wait for my call. I gave him a storybook and he left. The parents entered the room with eagerness.

"How is he?" the father asked.

"He is a good and a very bright kid. He misses his granddad a lot," I said calmly.

Both looked a bit surprised. They said he has passed away three years back. They were curious to know if Hero had said anything. I reassured them and explained to them *what a close relationship a child has with his grandparents.* It is a very special bond and they will miss them always. They did add that they had had a prayer gathering for him a few weeks back. I advised them to spend more time with the kid, talk to him before sleeping, as he needed *that* comfort from his family rather than toys or gadgets. They realized that they had been busy and had hardly spent time with him. It is just that he is busy juggling his classes and that he is tired; *this* was their understanding. I hinted to drop his drawing classes and that they should spend that time with him. He is good at drawing and it is a sheer waste of his energy.

Hero's father quickly said, "That is a great idea. I will adjust my office timings that day and come home early. Maybe I will join swimming with him or play badminton with him."

His wife looked at him with a surprised look, though her face lit up.

"So, with this sorted, may I call Hero inside? You all will discuss this at home in your own way, okay? This is your family thing and it should be a surprise for him, right!" after their unanimous nod, I called the receptionist and asked her to send Hero inside.

He entered the room with a big smile, as though he knew what had happened. I asked him to show his homework- "the menu thing". He looked shocked! He had forgotten and no one reminded him, he said, staring at his mom.

"We are eating now in the morning," his mom quickly said, and he joined, "Yes, mom gave me mini pizza yesterday and pasta today. I finished it, you can ask mom."

"I trust you, Hero, and believe in you. When you are saying you finished it then I am sure you must have finished it. Was it tasty?" I asked.

"Yummy! My mom makes the best food!" he exclaimed with joy.

With this, the session ended. Hero was given the same drawing homework and the parents were set on that secret mission.

Before closing the door, Hero whispered, "No more drawing classes, *na!*" with a big smile.

I just smiled and coincidently we both clapped silently. The door closed and the claps resounded in the room. Time to leave; my alarm went off. I had to make a call to inform my son that his playtime was over.

SESSION 3 & SESSION 4

The next two sessions took place on the following two Wednesdays. Hero was learning the coping skills well and he knew how to manage himself if he felt upset. I introduced some easy tips which he could follow in case he did not have his drawing copy with him. He applied them as a part of his homework and found it easy sometimes. He admitted at times he did not remember, which was absolutely okay. I eased out his anxiety and shared with him that it is normal for us to feel upset- the trick is to figure out how to react to it. We focused on the reaction part, discussed various ways in which he could react in different situations. He shared his own thoughts on how he could react at specific times, which was readily accepted by me. He completed his homework on time and always remembered to try any new skill he learned during the sessions. His school was going good, his sports activity was great and he had the football match on Monday (two days before our last session). He was very happy that his boring class was cancelled and instead his dad took special time out *just for him*. The happiness on his face and in his voice was beyond any measure. He loved the surprise given to him by his dad and positivity oozed out in every word he said. His granddad was also remembered on and off, and he was now calm whenever we said anything about him. His drawings were now more coherent with his stories. Dumbo also had a new friend, Tim, the great mouse. (Timothy, the mouse, is the friend in the story, Dumbo). We looked at each other and smiled when he said there is a friend of Dumbo's- the great mouse. In stories, anything and anyone can enter and leave, which gave the kids a sense of freedom and confidence.

The parents also made a conscious effort to spend quality time with their son and even arranged a surprise get-together for Hero. They ordered burgers, pizzas and ice-creams- *the so called junk food!* Hero was shocked and happy. They invited his building and school friends for lunch and played games with them. Everyone was happy and the family bonding grew stronger. It was challenging for the parents as they had to make a few changes in their work schedule; they managed and made it a point to inform their son when they got stuck in some work.

I informed Hero's parents and him that the next Wednesday would be his last session. Drawing homework was eased out; it was now optional. Everything was decided and the session time was fixed.

SESSION 5 – THE LAST SESSION

Hero was on time. He entered the room and was very excited. Before he could even sit he came near me and softly said, "We won!"

I was very happy and we both celebrated with our special claps. Somehow he managed to regain composure and started narrating details of the match. He blocked two goals which contributed to their victory and he won the *best player* prize. The joy and sense of achievement was contagious. He even ended up saying that he got superman powers because of the breakfast.

"I got full marks in my first term test except for in Hindi," he continued.

"Hindi needs practice, dear, it is a bit difficult."

"Not difficult at all, Ma'am, I got full in dictation. I was just lazy, I think," he said.

"Really, so now you have a plan?" keeping the momentum, I added quickly.

"Yes, I am going to practice every day and will do better the next time," he said. The self-realisation in Hero's attitude was a big change. He was responsible now and was able to communicate with his parents without thinking too much. He opened his drawing book. He said he wanted to go through each drawing with me. And the next few minutes were adorned with all the gizmo characters and situations. He laughed at some and even changed a few plots. I could see how the random thoughts were building into a systematic storyline. He even included his granddad in his story this time, along with football, his former math teacher, etc. Dumbo was no longer sad and had a smile when he sat alone with his book near the tree. It was his time and he was happy to be all by himself. We scanned through all the mini details and Hero was now ready to jump back into his chirpy world with energy.

He suddenly dived into his bag-pack and took out a piece of paper, folded neatly, and handed it to me. I smiled and took it, not knowing what it was. "It is for you, Ma'am," he said softly. His eyes were fixed at me and he sat very still observing me. I was under the spotlight now. I maintained my smile, as I opened the paper. A big *'Thank You'* was written on it and a few lines at the bottom of the page. The page was full of beautiful flowers and stars. I was surprised and instantly clapped, and with a broader smile said, "Thank you so much, Hero, this means a lot to me. You are a gem and you made my day. I will keep this very safely. It is just beautiful and very kind of you, dear. Indeed, I am very lucky NOW." He was very happy. He gave me a thumbs-up gesture and clapped; I joined in this celebration.

The few lines he wrote were, *'Ma'am, I miss my granddad, but now I know he is with me all the time. I am lucky and you also miss your granddad, now I know. Don't worry, Ma'am, I will tell you a story whenever you want and you are lucky too.'* A smiley face was drawn in the end.

This letter was very important. It shows the emotional maturity of a kid and that they do care for others. The thought that he conveyed to me was very strong. He also wanted to be of help to others, even an adult. I acknowledged his gesture and praised him for his thoughtfulness. He said that this letter is between us, a secret and that I can trust him. I smiled- these moments were added to my huge Pandora box of beautiful memories.

He knew this was his last session. As we discussed other things in his world including Ronaldo and Pokémon, I could see how he had progressed during these sessions.

"Can I come and meet you when I want to?" he asked.

"Yes, of course, Hero, you may come and meet me whenever you want to. Just send me a message and we may fix an appointment *especially for you*," I replied.

He seemed satisfied and started to keep his drawing book inside. I had a small gift for him.

I knew he liked Ronaldo so I gave him a book on Ronaldo. His jaw fell open as he unwrapped the gift paper quickly and saw Ronaldo on the cover page: 'Cristiano Ronaldo: The Ultimate Fan Book'. His happiness could not be contained in just a thank you; he kept on saying something or the other, as he flipped through the pages with eagerness.

Time ticked away pretty quickly and in no time his parents came to fetch him. As soon as he saw them he showed them the book, they smiled and said thank you. Hero was about to get busy in reading the book when I interrupted him. I told him this was his book and he may read it once he was home. This was a difficult task, indeed.

"Hero, I have another boy coming for a session after you leave. I don't want him to wait, *you* understand the importance of time, right!"- He quickly nodded- "Okay. So it is time to show your superpowers to everyone." He smiled, and then I addressed his parents, "I am happy that Hero has put an effort into whatever he was told to do with honesty. He is a bright kid and will do great in life. He can come and meet me, if the need arises, in the future," I said.

"We have a great time now. Thank you, madam," said Hero's father, looking at his son.

"Ma'am, *Hero has won the best player prize* and his studies have also improved," Hero's mother added.

They both praised their son and there were a few discussions- that he may slip at times, and that is okay; to pay attention to his diet- and they seemed satisfied. I was just a call away and they could take an appointment and come to meet me whenever they felt it was needed. With that, the session came to an end. Hero was very happy and held the book in his hand the entire time. Before disappearing, he gave that last special clap to me and smiled. I could hear his voice fading away in the corridor as he spoke about Ronaldo's goals. The place was full of happiness and contentment. I paused and prayed for his welfare. I had ten minutes for myself before the new client walked in.

Another leaf of another beautiful chapter. As I arranged the crayons and sheets of paper on the table, I saw the letter Hero gave me. I went through it again; it was truly heart-warming. I placed it safely in my drawer; the bell rang.

The receptionist informed me that the client had come. I told her to send them in. They knocked at the door-

"Come in!"

WHAT NEXT?

My next book, of course.

Part 2

In my upcoming book, I have the next age group that I want to draw your attention to, *The Teenagers and Young Adults (12 years – 25 years)*. This is the age when the pressure is on both the sides. The age range that I have selected is broad as I found that the emotional issues in this age group are similar. I have tried my best to depict personal counselling sessions with a young girl. Does she continue or leave the sessions midway? She seems to be on the brink of giving up hope. Her life is too demanding and this will drive her to ...

Remember some clients leave the sessions midway. They are gone without a word. We, as therapists, are not even aware of how they are once they leave. I do pray for each one of them but some need special mention.

Thanks a lot to all my readers for your valuable time. Your support does make a difference, and you can reach out to me in case of any concerns, feedback or assistance.

Thanks again for your support.

Contact Details

Email ID: hinabeg@yahoo.com

Contact Number: +91 9819495891

www.ingramcontent.com/pod-product-compliance
Lightning Source LLC
Chambersburg PA
CBHW051233250726
48655CB00006B/2749

* 9 7 8 1 6 4 6 7 8 8 1 0 1 *